The Basic Essentials of
CAMPING

by Cliff Jacobson

**Illustrations by
Cliff Moen**

ICS BOOKS, Inc.
Merrillville, Indiana

THE BASIC ESSENTIALS OF CAMPING

10 9 8 7

Printed in U.S.A.

DEDICATION

To my friend, Bob Brown, who continues to camp out but avowedly hates every minute of it!

ACKNOWLEDGMENTS

A special thanks to Dr. Bill Forgey, who at the start, believed in the idea of this book. To my editor, Tom Todd, who has always been willing to make last minute changes. And, to the following magazines for permission to use portions of my articles which appeared in their pages:

Canoe, October 1983: How to build a fire in the rain

Canoesport, 1987, for use of a portion of my "camping column."

Published by:
ICS BOOKS, Inc.
1370 E. 86th Place
Merrillville, IN 46410

recycled paper

Jacobson, Cliff.
    Camping : the basic essentials.

    (Basic essentials series)
    Includes index.
    1. Camping.   2. Camping—United States.   I. Title.
GV191.68.J327   1988   796.54'0973   88-2693
ISBN 0-934802-38-6

TABLE OF CONTENTS

Figure 1-1.

1. WHERE HAS ALL THE KNOW-HOW GONE?

I discovered the joys of camping at the age of 12 in a rustic Scout camp set deep in the Michigan woods. It was 1952, just before the dawn of nylon tents and 60/40 parkas. Aluminum canoes were hot off the Grumman forms, though I'd never seen one. Deep down, I believed they'd never replace the glorious Old Town's and Thompson's.

Like most kids my age, there was little money for outdoor gear. What I earned by picking pop bottles off the roadway went for a second-hand bike or a Randolph Scott movie. My camping outfit was carefully assembled from a rag-tag assortment of military surplus and Salvation Army store items. I knew only one kid who had equipment that was new. Once, I saved enough to buy an *"official"* Boy Scout knife, which in those days came with good carbon steel blades and a *metal* BSA insignia.

One Christmas, Dad gave me an all-steel Scout handaxe, which came complete with tooled leather sheath and varnished wood scales. For 20 years thereafter, I proudly carried it on all my hiking and canoe trips. It was my *"edge"* for making fires on a rainy day. Early on, I decided that those who badmouthed hatchets simply lacked the skills to use them right. Today, I retain that conviction, as you'll see in chapter 3.

1

On my fourteenth birthday, I received another treasured gift
— a solid brass M 71 Primus stove, which at five dollars, was a
genuinely expensive gift.

These items, plus an army surplus wool sleeping bag and
poncho, comprised my store of camping items. Everything fit nicely
into a tan canvas packsack and together tipped the scale at barely
20 pounds. To this, add a week's worth of dehydrated *"Seidel"*
trail foods, a handful of big stick matches and a spartan change of
clothes, and I was ready for the great adventure.

At last, I owned all the tripping gear I'd ever need. What boy
could be more fortunate? Admittedly, I yearned for an army down-
and-feathers sleeping bag — the wool one I had was adequate only
in the heat of summer. But no matter: With an extra blanket and
knitted sweater, I got by. Even in snow. After all, being a *"little
cold"* was part of the camping game, wasn't it?

My bible on how to camp was the *Boy Scout Handbook* which,
I was told, contained absolutely everything one could want to know
about the great outdoors. It was all there — from how to trench a
tent and build a bed of pine boughs, to the construction of rope-
lashed furniture and emergency dwellings. Axmanship was serious
stuff, so it was treated as a separate chapter.

Environmental concerns? There were none. Not that we didn't
care, you understand. We just didn't see anything wrong with
cutting trees and restructuring the soil to suit our needs. Reshaping
the land was, given the equipment of the day, the most logical way
to make outdoor life bearable.

Litter, of course, was another matter. We proudly packed out
everything we (and anyone else) brought in. We were Boy Scouts,
not slobs!

In 1958, Calvin Rutstrum brought out his first book, *The Way
Of The Wilderness*. Suddenly, there was new philosophy afield.
Calvin knew the days of trenched tents and bough beds were num-
bered. His writings challenged readers to *"think before they cut,"*
to use an air mattress instead of a spruce bed. Wilderness camping
was in proud transition. New products — nylon, dacron, stainless
steel and vinyl were already fractionating the monopolies enjoyed
by cotton, wool and canvas. Outfitters by the thousands sold (or

burned!) their cotton tents and joined the nylon revolution.

Suddenly, the emphasis had shifted from *"skills"* to *"things."* Knowing how was no longer good enough. Everyone needed a plethora of new gear — down sleeping bags and foam sleeping pads; Swiss army knives with a tool for everything; waterproof boots with vibram lugs; two piece rain suits with clever hoods that moved with the turn of a head; polypropylene socks and underwear and pile pullovers; erector-set tents that needed no staking; Gore-tex suits that *"breathed"* in the rain; color-matched designer clothes that looked good at the All-Stars game. And tiny trail stoves that ran on canisters of liquid butane.

Suddenly I felt quite inadequate, like a peasant in Camelot.

The late Calvin Rutstrum summed it up one foggy morning on a mid-September day. I'd driven up to meet him at his wilderness cabin on the Lake Superior north shore. Cal had built the place himself, every inch of it. No need to pour a concrete slab; a mirror flat shelf of slate was good enough. The double cabin was artfully constructed from native pines. And it was solid!

As Cal poured coffee, I baited him by pulling from its stuff sack a polyester-filled sleeping bag I'd purchased for my wife.

"Whatcha think of these new poly bags?" I asked. *"They dry really fast — could be a lifesaver if you get your down bag wet."*

With that, Rutstrum, in his early eighties, slammed down his cup on the wood-pinned table and splashed brown liquid onto the varnished wood. Slowly, he rose, his set jaw and steel gray eyes poised in anger.

"Damn!" he called loudly: *"I've canoed and camped for nigh on 70 years and I've never gotten my down bag wet. Never. Not ever! Those who get stuff wet on a trip need help. They need to learn how to camp ...!"*

I could have cheered!

Seems as though high tech gear and high-powered salesmanship have become a substitute for rock solid camping skills. Chemical fire-starters take the place of correct fire making; *"indestructible"* canoes are the solution to hitting rocks; blizzard-proof tents become the answer to one's inability to stormproof conventional designs. And the *"What if you get your down bag wet"* syndrome attracts new converts each year. In the end, only the manufacturers win. For even the best gear falls short of expectations without proper know-how.

And that, friends, is what this book is all about. No pressure to buy the new, discard the old. Just a mash of proven procedures to enhance your camping trips.

2. HOW TO USE YOUR GEAR EFFECTIVELY

I recently checked the contents of a popular backpacking book and found that around 90 percent of its pages were devoted to the selection of equipment. There were full chapters on *"Choosing the sleeping bag," "A tent for all seasons,"* and *"Getting booted up."* Except for some obvious advice about pitching camp on high ground, and packing clothes in waterproof bags, there was precious little of value to crow about. Right then, I vowed to take a more practical tack in THE BASIC ESSENTIALS OF CAMPING.

Certainly, proper equipment is important to a quality outdoor experience. Only a fool would suggest otherwise. But the engineering specifics of every product are available free from the manufacturer, and detailed equipment evaluations are the annual rule in most every outdoor magazine. And if you're still confused over what variables go into selecting a great tent or sleeping bag, just ask the folks who sell outdoor gear at first- rate camping shops. Most of these young men and women are quite knowledgeable. All are active hikers, bikers, canoeists and skiers (they wouldn't have gotten the job, otherwise!) High-tech camping equipment is not usually sold on commission, which means the purveyors will react honestly to your concerns.

So rather than clutter this chapter with equipment trivia that is readily available elsewhere, I'll suggest some ways to make your good gear perform at its best. Appendix 1 contains the general check lists you need to make initial purchases.

Sleeping Bags

What you choose depends on how classy you want to travel and how much you want to spend. At the top of the list are 300 dollar down bags, while at the bottom are 29 dollar *"astro-fill"* specials which are no better than paired blankets. And speaking of blankets: A set of airy acrylic or loose woven wool blankets, sandwiched ala boy scout style (Figure 2-1) makes a perfectly good bed for typical summer campouts. If cost *is* an object, here's the place to cut. There's no sense buying three season protection if

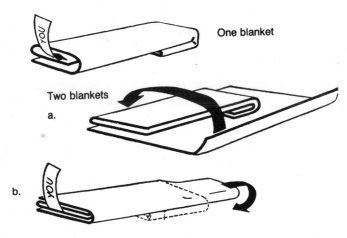

Figure 2-1. For summer use, blankets will work as well as a sleeping bag. Here's how to fold them for maximum warmth.

you'll use it only in the blistering heat of summer. Most campers own bags which are too warm. Only if you're heading to the far north should you consider the merits of an autumn rated (25 degree Fahrenheit) sleeping bag.

For car camping (which really can't be called *"sleeping out"*), any sleeping bag will do. Otherwise, my vote goes to a *roomy* mummy bag with a fully formed head and boxed (raised) foot. Be sure the bag has a *two way* zipper that runs from foot to chin.

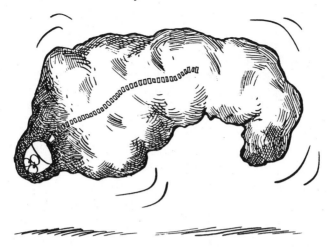

Figure 2-2. Be sure it has a full length zipper which runs from foot to chin.

In sleeping bags, more than any other camping product, you get exactly what you pay for. At this writing, a C-note will put you into a quality synthetic bag. Twice this will buy a good down bag.

So which one for you? First, be aware that *good* down will outlast the best Polarguard/Hollofil/Quallofil by *decades*. Conscientious bag makers suggest a *"useful"* life of around five years for a heavily used synthetic bag. With down bags, the nylon shell goes first. How long? Well, one of my down bags is now 20 years old and it's still going strong!

As to the argument that down bags are hard to dry when they get wet on a camping trip, rethink the logic of Calvin Rutstrum. If you pack your bag as I suggest, you'll never get it wet. Not ever!

Packing the Sleeping Bag

The recommended procedure for waterproofing the sleeping bag is to stuff it into a nylon sack that has first been lined with a plastic bag. This is foolish advice! For everytime you *"stuff"* the bag into the plastic sack, you stretch and abraid the plastic. In no time, tears — and leaks — develop. Some experts know this and so suggest that you carry *"some extra plastic bags,"* which is even more absurd.

Here's a better way: First, stuff the bag into its nylon sack (which need not be watertight), then set the sack inside a sturdy plastic bag. Pleat and twist the end of the plastic bag, fold it over and secure it with a loop of shock-cord. Then, place this unit into an oversize nylon sack (again, which need not be waterproof). Note that the delicate plastic liner — which is the only real water barrier — is protected from abrasion on *both* sides!

It's especially important to adopt this procedure if you'll be tying your sleeping bag onto the outside of a pack frame where it will be constantly exposed to the weather. You'll also appreciate the extra abrasion resistance of the sandwiched construction when you hike through thorns or brambles. On one occasion, I sliced through an outer stuff sack while hiking in rough country.

In camp: Some authorities advise you to lay out your sleeping bag and fluff it to full loft well in advance of bed time. This is supposed to increase its insulative value. Hogwash! Better to leave the bag stuffed and protected until you need it. A good sleeping bag will fluff to full loft within 60 seconds after it's pulled from the sack. Just give it a good shake before you climb in.

Washing Your Sleeping Bag

First, never dry clean your sleeping bag — down or synthetic. Handwashing is the recommended procedure, though machine washing, *in a front loader only* (!), works just as well.

As to soaps, *any* liquid detergent will do. Powdered detergents are okay if you can get them to dissolve thoroughly.

Here are the rules:

1.   Use warm or cold water only. Excess heat will destroy any sleeping bag!

2.   Use *half as much* liquid detergent as you think you need. I've had good luck with Ivory Liquid, Joy, Palmolive, and Basic H.

3.   Remove the spun-dry bag from the washer and place it in an extractor (a high speed centrifuge, available at laundromats). One pass through the extractor will remove nearly all the water.

4.   Dry the bag at *low* heat setting in a large commercial dryer. Be sure the dryer actually puts out *low* heat. If it doesn't, jam a magazine over the safety button so you can run the door ajar. Note: a terry cloth towel placed in the dryer with the sleeping bag will speed drying.

That's all there is to it! I wash my sleeping bags once a year.

Tent

You don't need a sophisticated high-altitude tent for general camping. Any simple forest tent will do if it has a bathtub floor (no perimeter seams at ground level) and a waterproof fly that stakes nearly to the ground. The fly must cover *every* seam and floor corner! If you rely on glue (seam sealant) to waterproof exposed seams, you're just asking for trouble! A vestibule (alcove) is important: It provides a place to store equipment out of the weather. Vestibules also seal the entryway of a tent from blowing rain and snow.

Size: Each person needs about 2 1/2 by 7 feet just to stretch out. Add an additional half foot (3' x 7') plus headroom enough to dress, and you enter the realm of comfort. A tent used for general camping should be relatively commodius — a 6 foot by 8 foot floor plan (commonly referred to as a 3-4 person tent) is ideal for two. Weight? Under 12 pounds, and the lighter the better. Serious backpackers will opt for the lightest, most compact tent they can get, which may or may not be a good idea. If you have to spend the day weather-bound in a doghousy little shelter with no room to sit upright, you'll wish you'd brought a bigger tent! Your tent is your home away from home. This is not the place to cut corners.

You'll pay much more for high-tech geometrics (domes, tunnels and such) than for simple-to-sew but reliable A-frames. If you're going to the mountains and need the reliability of a windproof tent, by all means get one. But if your camping will be confined to the tree line, choose a more *"moderate"* design — one which enables you to keep your sanity in an all day rain.

Don't leave home without installing a plastic groundcloth *inside* your tent. The groundsheet will prevent pooled surface water which wicks through floor seams (and in time, worn floor fabric) from entering your sleeping area. *Don't* place the plastic sheet under the tent as advised by some tentmakers — rain water may become trapped between it and the floor and be pressure-wicked (from body weight) through the nylon fabric into the tent. You'll really have a sponge party if this happens! Use of an *interior* groundcloth is the best wet-weather tip I can give you. On numerous occasions, this feature has saved me from an unexpected midnight bath.

Almost any tent can be made to survive a severe storm, if you know how to rig it. Chapter 7 shows you how.

Clothing and Raingear

You don't need outdoor designer wear to enjoy camping. Simply avoid wearing cotton, except in the height of summer heat, and you'll do fine. Blue jeans are a particularly bad choice: Once they get wet and cold, they stay that way. A number of deaths due to hypothermia (more on that later) have been traced to the wearing of this article.

A lot of very experienced campers do all their shopping at army surplus and discount stores, where they find good quality items at low prices. Military woolens, inexpensive acrylics and polyester pile are the favored regimen, as are cotton/polyester fatigues and *"chinos."*

A breathable nylon jacket is essential to stem the biting winds, and don't forget polypropylene or wool long johns when the need arises. A change of clothes from nose to toes is the rule whether you're going for a weekend or a month. Everything should fit easily into an 8-inch by 11-inch nylon stuff sack.

Rain gear should be uncomplicated. A two-piece rain suit is better than a poncho, which dribbles through, or a knee-length shirt (cagoule), which is awkward for everything except lazing about camp. The best buys on rainwear are usually found in industrial supply stores where construction workers shop. The new construction-grade rain suits are strong, light, and wondrously inexpensive. They'll keep you plenty dry even though they lack the exquisite tailoring, multiple pockets and exotic hoods (which you really don't need) of high-tech camp store garments.

Do not wear your rain gear for wind protection, as is commonly advised. Any item that is frequently worn will eventually develop holes. Wear your nylon shell jacket for wind and keep the poly-coated stuff for its intended purpose. *Always* store rain clothes in a nylon sack to eliminate the abrasion that results from stuffing these garments into packsacks.

What you wear *under* raingear is important. A light polypropylene or wool shirt will eliminate the clammy feeling which results from wearing waterproof clothing next to the skin.

And what about Gore-tex? Gore-tex garments are purported to be *"waterproof and breathable."* They are. Sometimes. My own experience with this product suggests it is perfectly adequate for the kind of light camping most people do. Unfortunately, I've seen Gore-tex fail often enough on extended trips that I'm not yet willing to trust it when the chips are down.

So you're taking the children: No sense spending a bundle on clothing that will be outgrown in a season. *Acrylics* are the key word here. They are very inexpensive and dry almost instantly after a rain. A light, non-allergenic acrylic sweater worn next to the skin makes a fine underwear top for chilly weather. Again, avoid blue jeans: Cotton/polyester slacks dry faster and are cheaper. Rain gear is easy: A cut down plastic poncho worn over a waterproof nylon jacket (double protection plus dry sleeves) will keep a youngster dry in the worst storms. Add a plastic souwester hat and rubber boots, and your little one is set for a delightful day afield.

Footwear

The trend is to very lightweight boots for all but the most demanding applications. No knowledgeable hiker I know would be caught dead wearing the five pound Vibram lug monstrosities which were so popular a decade ago. Now, footwear rules are simple: Wear the lightest most flexible boot you can find. Exceptions are mountaineering and winter travel. If you need a really waterproof shoe, go for all-rubber or shoe-pac (leather top/rubber bottom) construction.

Here's an easy way to break in leather boots: Fill each boot with luke warm tap water and allow the water to sit in the boot no more than 15 seconds. Pour out the water then walk the boots dry. Afterwards, rub in a generous amount of leather preservative. Clean your boots regularly with saddle soap, and re-apply preservative as needed.

Wear *two* pairs of socks in your boots. The outer pair should be made from heavy wool (at least 75 percent); the inner pair of lightweight wool or polypropylene (these are marvelous!). Wear the light liners *inside out* so that seams are away from your foot. This one precaution will eliminate most blisters. Liners should be changed daily. Outer socks may be worn two or three days, depending on your level of activity.

Packs

What you need depends entirely on your tripping style. For backpacking on relatively good trails, the aluminum frame outfit reigns supreme. Rock scrambling requires more dexterity; hence, the development of the *"soft pack"* with internal stays. And for canoeing, nothing beats the venerable Duluth pack, which is nothing more than a canvas envelope with three closing straps. There are also a number of specialized packsacks which are designed for technical rock climbing and day meandering. The salespeople at any good equipment store will overwhelm you with the specifics of design and fit.

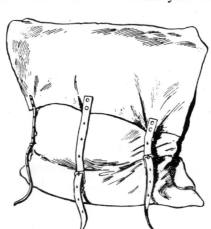

Figure 2-3. The Duluth pack, a canvas envelope which measures 24 by 30 inches, is the preferred pack for canoeing.

How to pack your pack: Now that most packs come with internal or external frames, the science of *"proper packing"* has all but vanished. And that's too bad because there is an efficient way to do things.

Proper packing begins with effective waterproofing. Now write this in technicolor: *Regardless of the manufacturer's claims, my pack IS NOT waterproof!* Even double coated pack fabrics are not foolproof. After all, there are seams. And fabrics do wear. The slightest scratch will allow a leak.

So start by lining your pack with a large plastic bag. Inside this, place a light fabric abrasion liner of some sort. The liner need not be waterproof — shear polypropylene or nylon taffeta will do. Its only purpose is to absorb the abrasion which results from stuffing gear deep into the pack. The *"sandwich"* principle is the same as that recommended for packing the sleeping bag.

Exterior pack pockets must also be waterproofed. Zip-lock bags are one solution; the pack rain coat — a tailored poly-coated nylon apron which fits over the pack — is another. In camp, a giant plastic garbage bag will protect everything from the worst rain.

Principles of packing: For general hiking, you want the weight as close to your back and as high as possible. This means the sleeping bag and foam pad go on the bottom, followed by clothing and sundries. Reserve the top shelf for food, tent and cooking gear.

Rock scrambling demands a lower load, though one which still hugs your body. Frameless packs are best loaded flat (horizontally) to assure that soft items are evenly distributed along the back and not massed together where they'll do no good.

Packing the tent: Here's your most obstinate load: Invariably the poles will be too long to fit in the pack. Most hikers respond by simply setting the lengthy tent bag under the closing flap of their packsack, which is hardly a good idea for these reasons: 1) It raises the load too high, which may unbalance the hiker; 2) The tent is exposed to the elements and thorny vegetation; 3) Rain can get into the pack by working its way under the badly sealed closing flap.

Far better to pack tent and poles *separately* as follows:

1.   Stuff (my preference) or roll the tent, without stakes and poles, and place it in an *oversize* nylon bag. Pack poles and stakes

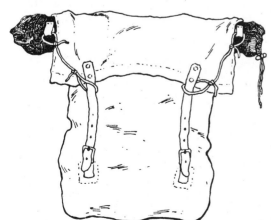

Figure 2-4. Pack the tent and poles separately. Set the *pole and stake bag* just under the pack flap and run the closing straps of the pack flap through loops of nylon cord sewn to the ends of the pole bag.

in a separate nylon bag with drawstring closure.

2.   Pack the tent between the waterproof plastic pack liner and the tightly rolled fabric abrasion liner. This will isolate it from the dry gear below. Set the pole and stake bag just under the pack flap and run the closing straps of the pack flap through loops of nylon cord sewn to the ends of the pole bag (or simply tie these cords to the pack frame).

3.   Cinch the pack flap down tightly. The nylon cords keep the pole bag from sliding out beneath the pack flap.

Rain Fly (Tarp)

A 10-foot by 10-foot nylon rain tarp, tightly pitched between two trees, will enable you to prepare meals, make repairs, and otherwise enjoy a rainy day. The rain tarp is one of the most essential and overlooked items on a camping trip. Chapter 7 provides an in-depth look at how to rig it.

Stove

Essential in all but the most infrequented areas. I prefer the self-contained single burner gasoline models, through the small two burner Colemans are your best buy. The stove is so important, I've allotted a full chapter to it.

Toys

A butane lighter, flashlight, Sierra cup for a ladle, pot lifter or pliers, duct tape, rope and parachute cord, and a miniature sewing kit will suffice for the short trip. Extended stays require a full battery of supportive toys — everything from instant epoxy to leather replacement gaskets for the stove.

It's impossible to describe all you need to have — and need to know — in a chapter of this length. So don't neglect your studies. Read every book on camping you can find before you take to the backcountry, and keep abreast of new developments by attending outdoor seminars. After all, it's one thing to own good gear; it's another to know how to use it effectively!

3. THE CUTTING EDGE

In the 1920's there was the sheath knife and full size axe. By 1950, the common jack knife and three-quarter length axe was in vogue. The seventies brought forth the yuppie movement, and with it, the red-handled Swiss army knife. Now, the trend is to giant lock-back folders and no axe at all.

Somewhere in their vacillation, campers have overlooked an important fact: Slicing cheese, splitting kindling and other knife related chores are about the same today as a century ago. It follows then that your choice of edged tools should — with appropriate modifications — reflect these similarities.

Here's my formula for a *"camp knife."*

1.   Enough length (4-5 inch blade) to slice meat and cheese and reach deep into the peanut butter jar without getting gunked up.

2.   A thin, flat-ground blade for effortless slicing.

Nearly all knives sold for outdoor use have blades which are too thick. One-eighth of an inch across the spine is the *maximum* thickness permissible for a utility knife, no matter how delicate the edge. Try slicing a tomato with the typical hunting knife and you'll see why!

The primary camp knife may be a fixed blade or folding model. You'll pay more for a good folder than for a sheath knife of similar length.

If your taste runs to folding knives, select a model with a 3 to 4-inch long, *thin,* flat-ground blade. If you want a razor-sharp edge that's easy to maintain, choose carbon steel over stainless. The best stainless blades are very good but they can't compare to good tool steel knives for ease-of-sharpening and holding an edge.

Invariably, you'll need two knives for camping — a thin-ground kitchen style model for preparing foods, and a substantial multi-purpose folder of some sort. In case you're wondering, my favorite camp knife is a Gerber Shorty — a wafer-thin hunting knife with 4 1/2-inch flat-ground blade.

Sharpening: Never use an electrical sharpener or one of those mechanical wheeled gadgets sold at supermarkets. You'll ruin the knife beyond repair! Instead, get a synthetic diamond stone (first choice) and/or a medium grit *soft* Arkansas stone. If you want the finest razor edge, obtain a *hard* Arkansas stone as well.

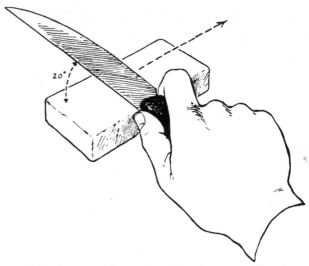

Figure 3-1. Maintain a 15-20 degree angle, and cut *into* the stone. Use plenty of cutting oil and clean the stone (and blade) frequently.

Maintain a light film of cutting oil on the natural stones (use water on diamond stones) to float away steel particles. Raise the back of the blade 15-20 degrees and cut *into* the stone, as illustrated.

Clean the stone and blade frequently and apply new oil during the sharpening process. I generally take four strokes per side and apply new oil (first, cleaning off the old) every 30 strokes or so. When sharpening is complete, I strop the blade on leather to produce a razor-fine edge.

The Hand Axe

It's almost impossible to maintain a bright fire after a week long rain without a wood splitting tool of some sort. A big axe is fine if weight is no object and you've got the space to carry it. Otherwise, a high quality all-steel hand axe will suffice. Despite what you may have read and heard about the dangers of hatchets, they are really quite safe if you follow the guidelines below. When used along with a folding saw, a hand axe will produce all the camp wood you need, with surprisingly little effort.

To avoid "axidents," follow these rules:

1. *Saw* wood to be split into 12 inch lengths.

2. Use the hand axe as a *splitting wedge: Do not* chop with it! The folding saw performs *all* cutting functions.

3. Set the axe head lightly into the end grain of the wood (Figure 3-2). One person holds the tool while a friend pounds it through with a chunk of log. All-steel hand axes are better for this

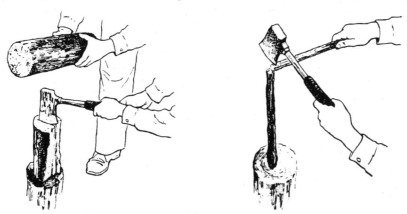

Figure 3-2. Splitting wood is easy if you use the axe as a splitting wedge rather than a "chopping" tool. Thick logs can be split by this method.

Figure 3-3. Kindling splits easier from the end grain — a process that is made easier (and safer!) if you use a stick of wood to hold the upright piece in place.

than those with wooden handles as they are less likely to break. When splitting very thick (over 6-inches) logs, take multiple splitting off the edges.

Caution: Hold the axe solidly with *both* hands. Allow the log hammer to do all the work.

To produce kindling: Kindling splits easiest from the end grain, a process that's made easier and safer if you use a stick of wood to hold the upright in place (Figure 3-3).

Sharpening the axe: Remove nicks with a flat mill file. True the edge with a diamond stone or soft Arkansas stone. Leave a coating of oil on the blade to resist rust.

Folding Saw

This tool is a must for making fire on a rainy day! Steel-framed bow saws are sturdy (fine for car camping) but they don't pack well. Aluminum-framed folding saws are flimsy and their triangular shapes don't permit you to cut big logs. Best camp saw I've seen is a full-stroke rectangular model called the FAST BUCKSAW. It's constructed of hard maple and has an easily replaceable 21-inch blade (re-fills are available at any hardware store). When assembled, it's so rigid you'd swear it was a one-piece model. These saws are available by mail from Fast Bucksaw, Inc., 110 E. Fifth St., Hastings, MN 55033.

4. TO BUILD A FIRE!

The ability to make fire when the woods are drenched from rain is one of the most difficult and important of all outdoor tasks. Yet it is a skill which few people possess. Here's how to get the job done quickly and efficiently, regardless of the whims of nature.

Some years ago, after a gentle rain, I watched for an hour while two teen-agers tried to build a campfire. The boys struck match after match without success, ultimately giving up in disgust. Casually, I strolled over, rearranged a few pieces of wood, and with a single match, set the mass aflame. As the youngsters looked on in awe, I dismissed the whole thing by suggesting it was my *"flaming personality"* that provided the edge.

After witnessing scores of similar episodes, I conclude that while anyone can make fire on a sun-scorched day, precious few have the ability when the weather deteriorates to persistent rain.

Skeptical? Stroll around a state park campground after a tingling thundershower and count the number of fires you see burning brightly ... compared to the amount of wet gear hanging hopelessly out to dry.

Wilderness guidebooks suggest that a knowledgeable woodsman can start a fire with a single match instantly in a major storm. Hardly! No one can make fire reliably under these conditions, but anyone can succeed in a moderate downpour or week-long drizzle, if he or she *"knows how."*

"Know-how" begins with the right tinder, and to come up with that, you'll need the right tools: A folding saw, small hand axe (hatchet), and a sharp knife — hence the importance of the previous chapter.

Now for that tinder. In the north country, the tendency is to search for birchbark — much to the detriment of the birch trees and displeasure of campers who may later occupy the site. Besides, any birchbark you find during or immediately after a good soaking rain is probably too wet to burn anyway. And on a dry day, there are better alternatives.

Instead, seek out the dead, pencil-thin branches near the base of evergreen trees. These shade-killed twigs are protected from rain by the tree canopy and are usually bone-dry. They'll break with a crisp snap even after days of prolonged rain. If the branches are wet to the touch but you can hear the *"snap,"* the wood's dry enough to burn. A handful of this tinder is all you need.

If evergreen twigs are rain-soaked or unavailable (and in state parks they *are not* available!), locate a log with a dry center. Search the *open areas* of your campsite for a length of jutting birch, pine, cedar, or other softwood. When you find one of these *"blowdowns"* poking into the clearing, saw off the section that doesn't touch the land. Some basic biology here: You'll find deadfalls in the woods as well as in the open, but they're often rotten from the dampness of the forest — and rotten wood, as everyone knows, burns poorly. However, snags which protrude from the forest are flooded with sunlight (which kills most decay-causing microorganisms) and so are more apt to have sound, dry wood inside.

Saw the sun-lit section of log into 12-inch lengths and split and sliver it with the hand axe by the method outlined in chapter three.

Next, slice long thin slivers of wood from the heartwood split-tings. This is your tinder. When you have plenty of tinder on hand, build your fire step-by-step.

Step One
Set two one inch diameter sticks parallel to one another, about

six inches apart. Place a few pencil-thin pieces of kindling over them at right angles. Space the pieces of kindling about an inch apart.

Step Two

Carefully place long, thin shavings or small dry twigs (tinder) on top of the kindling. Don't crowd the tinder; the fire must have adequate ventilation to burn properly.

Next, put two sticks about one-half inch in diameter over the ends of the inch-thick sticks at right angles to the fire base. These sticks will support the heavier kindling which you will pile atop the shavings.

Step Three

When you've stacked the shavings about an inch high, weight them in place (so the wind won't blow them away) with several criss-crossed pencil-thin sticks. Follow this with a few larger pieces of wood. For best results, use split kindling rather than sticks gathered from the forest floor.

Your fire is now ready to light! It will start with a single match.

The procedure I've outlined is time-consuming but foolproof. The unique construction of the fire guarantees success because:

1. The match is applied directly below the tinder in keeping with the principle that heat (and flame) goes upward, not sideways. Typical campfires are ordinarily ignited along one edge.

2. The tinder box is elevated which produces an efficient chimney-like draft. The rich, smoke-free flame of the young blaze gains momentum quickly.

3. The tinder doesn't touch the cold, damp ground.

Figure 4-1. For best results, your fire set should look like this.

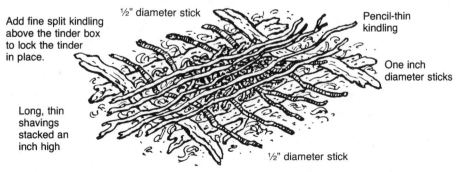

Add fine split kindling above the tinder box to lock the tinder in place.

½" diameter stick

Pencil-thin kindling

One inch diameter sticks

Long, thin shavings stacked an inch high

½" diameter stick

Tips

In the piney woods of the North and East, look for the balsam fir tree. Its sap is nearly as volatile as kerosine. In summer, the tree produces half-dollar sized resin blisters on its trunk. Lance a few blisters with a sharp stick and collect the pitch on a piece of wood or bark. Set the *"resin cup"* directly under your fire base and light it. Voilá! Fire every time — with one match.

Carry a butane lighter and save matches for emergencies. Also, bring a candle plus some *"Fire Ribbon"* or other chemical fire-starter. For trips where a quick warming fire may be required, assemble these kit materials: A flattened half-gallon milk carton, a handful of thick shavings, and some splittings of scrap wood. Put everything into a nested pair of plastic bags.

When the emergency strikes, dump everything on the ground, frizz up the milk carton and splash it with *"Fire Ribbon."* Light the Ribbon and toss all the wood on top. The carton will burn for about three minutes, the wood an additional five. That's enough time for you to search the woods for more fuel while your wet friend is being re-warmed by your instant blaze.

Let's review the rules for making a successful fire:

1.   Place sticks far enough apart on the fire base so there'll be adequate ventilation for the developing flames. The most common reason for fire failure is *lack of oxygen.*

2.   Tinder should be no larger in diameter than the thickness of a match. Trying to ignite wood larger than that on a damp day is a waste of time.

3. Don't heap the fire base high with wood during the developing stages of the flame. Unnecessary fuel just draws heat from the young fire and cools it. Pre-set pyramid-style fires (ala Boy Scouts) look nice in handbooks but burn inefficiently. Once you complete Step 3, wood should be added one stick at a time and placed strategically so you can *"see light"* between each one. Smoke is nature's way of telling you you're suffocating the blaze.

Extinguishing the blaze: It should go without saying that your fire *must* be dead out when you leave your campsite. The rules are simple: When the smoke is gone and you have thoroughly doused everything with water, *check the fire with your hands.* If it's hot enough to burn your fingers, it's hot enough to burn a forest!

5. CHOOSING A CAMP STOVE

You can, of course, cook everything over an open fire. And a lot of campers do just that. But maintaining a cooking fire in the typical state park campground — where wood must be purchased at a dollar a bundle — is comparable to burning money. In the deep backcountry, a stove is less essential, for good wood is readily found. If, however, you've driven many miles to a favorite wilderness and found a fire ban in effect, you'll wish you'd brought a stove!

. **A Summary of Stove Types**

There are gasoline, kerosene, butane and propane stoves. Only gasoline and kerosene — and for car campers, propane — stoves make much sense.

Figure 5-2. PEAK 1 Stove: Gasoline stoves are the most reliable of the pack.

Gasoline stoves are the most reliable of the pack, especially in bad weather. And gasoline has the highest heat output of all stove fuels. Generally, gasoline stoves accept only *"white gas"* or Coleman fuel (highly refined forms of naptha). It's not safe to burn leaded gasoline in them. An important distinction must be made between additive-free white gasoline — which is difficult to obtain — and additive-packed automotive *"unleaded gasoline"* which is available at every gas station. Unleaded gas is more volatile than white gas and may produce excessive pressures in stoves designed for white gas only.

Kerosene has about the same BTU rating as gasoline but it's less volatile. Where a gasoline stove will explode, a kerosene one will simply burn. But kerosene stoves are smelly and they must be primed with alcohol or gasoline. Nonetheless, they are very safe and are grand for camp cooking.

Propane is relatively inexpensive and it puts out good heat.

Its big drawback is in the packaging: The heavy steel cylinders which contain the gas are fine in a Vanbago but not in the packsack of a hiker or canoeist.

Butane stoves are cutesy affairs which light with the turn of an adjuster knob. They need no pumping, priming or filling. Refueling takes seconds and consists of merely snapping on a new gas cylinder. But butane stoves put out little heat: The colder it gets the less flame they manage. At around freezing, they quit working altogether. You won't find experienced campers using butane stoves. They're fine for the yuppie crowd and for high altitude work where the gas develops sufficient pressures. For all around camping, there are better alternatives.

Stove Features

Stability: There's nothing more frustrating than simmering a big pot of spaghetti on a precarious little beast that wobbles with every stir of the spoon. Before you buy, remember that some stoves which look great in the store, tip over in the field!

Ease-of-starting: Stoves that come equipped with built-in pumps start faster and generally put out more heat than those without pumps. For general camping, a pump is a must.

Susceptibility to wind: The first time you've got to build a rock wall around your stove to keep it perking you'll understand the value of a good windscreen. Avoid stoves with thin aluminum windscreens that burn up, and detachable ones which can be lost.

An adjustable flame: If you intend to fry pancakes or simmer stew, you'll want an infinitely adjustable flame — a feature most compact trail stoves don't have. The venerable Coleman twin burner and compact PEAK 1 offer the finest adjustments of any stoves currently available.

Here are some *"Do's and don'ts"* that will keep your camp stove perking merrily season after season.

DO'S

DO carry fuel only in recommended containers. Volatiles are best transported in aluminum liter bottles or in the original steel can.

DO frequently check the temperature of your stove's fuel tank by feeling it with your hand. If the tank is too hot to hold, reduce the stove's heat and/or pour cold water on the tank.

DO carry extra stove parts and tools. An extra pressure cap and leather pump washer is usually enough. Bring a small screwdriver and pliers.

DO empty the fuel in your stove at the end of each season. Impurities in fuel left in stoves can cause malfunctions. Note: This is the most common cause of long term stove failure!

DON'TS

DON'T loosen or remove the filler cap of a gasoline stove when the stove is burning. This could result in an explosion!

DON'T re-fuel a hot stove. There may be sufficient heat still available to ignite the gas fumes.

DON'T set over-size pots on stoves. Large pots reflect excessive heat back to the fuel tank, which may cause overheating of the stove. Run stove at three-fourths of maximum heat output if you use oversize pots.

DON'T use automotive gasoline (regular or unleaded) in a stove designed to burn white gas.

DON'T start a stove inside a tent or confined area; the resulting flare-up can be dangerous.

DON'T operate any stove where there is insufficient ventilation. A closed tent is not sufficiently ventilated!

DON'T set stoves on sleeping bags or tent floors. There's enough heat generated at the base of some stoves to melt or warp these items.

DON'T run stoves at full power for extended periods of time. The tank may overheat and cause the safety valve to blow.

DON'T enclose a stove with aluminum foil to increase its heat output. The stove may overheat and explode!

DON'T fill gasoline or kerosene stoves more than three-fourths full. Fuel won't vaporize if there's insufficient room for it to expand.

6. TASTY ROUTES TO DINING OUT

There are two schools of thought about camp cooking: One prefers spending whatever time is required to make delicious meals, even if it means sweating for hours over a smoky fire and dutch oven. The other view goes something like this: *"Since I spend only about a week a year in the outdoors, I like to keep foods simple. If it takes more than 20 minutes to prepare, forget it!"*

I prefer the latter approach, as the following example illustrates: Some years ago, after a gentle rain, I went for an evening paddle along the shore of a popular lake in the Boundary Waters Canoe Area. As I rounded a point, I happened upon a man and woman sitting contentedly on a rock ledge, staring into the star-lit sky. I paddled over and struck up a conversation, in the course of which I asked: *"How come you folks don't have a bright cheery fire going?"*

With this, the man began his story. He and his wife were newcomers to the backcountry — neither had canoed or camped before. They arranged to have an outfitter supply all their needs, and he reciprocated by providing a wealth of slow cook foods. There were pancakes and french toast for breakfast, grilled cheese sandwiches and soup for lunch, and multi-course dried foods for supper — all of which required a well maintained fire or stove (which the couple didn't have) to prepare.

27

Figure 6-1. BLAH — we added soap not soup!

"For the first three days we followed the menu," said the man. *"We got up early and built our cooking fire; stopped at noon and built another. It was a hassle. By the end of the third day we had covered only 15 miles. Then the rains hit and we couldn't start a fire. So we pulled out all the dried stuff — crackers and cheese, peanut butter and jelly, etc. With no fires to slow us down, we began making time. We started averaging 15 miles a day instead of 5. Now, we're seeing the country — and that's what we came here for!"*

When I offered to show the couple how to make a wet-weather fire, they politely declined, reaffirming their commitment to the joys of efficient traveling.

Admittedly, PBJ's and cold cheese sandwiches are not my cup of tea, even on a fast-paced camping trip. I prefer a more middle ground approach — a reasonably quick breakfast, no cook lunch, and a lazy but determined supper. Some of my favorite trail meals are listed below:

Breakfast — Requires only boiling water
Instant Oatmeal (Maple and brown sugar flavor is most popular)
Small package of raisins
A chunk of hard sausage or a few sticks of beef jerky
Instant orange drink
Tea or coffee

Slow Cook Breakfast
Flap jacks with hot syrup and melted margarine
Canned or slab bacon
Orange drink
Toasted bagel
Coffee or tea

Lunches
Except when I operate out of a base camp, I prefer lunches which need no cooking. Invariably, my meals tend to be nutritious but spartan, and center around these ingredients:
Pita (Mediterranean pocket) bread — keeps at least a week without refrigeration.
Assorted cheeses and hard sausage
Granola bars
Peanut butter and jelly
Wylers or Kool-Aid instant fruit drink
Hard candies

Suppers
After two very predictable meals, supper is a blessing. Often, I get quite extravagant, relying on canned sauces and fresh vegetables to spark life into the menu. Instant Lipton and Knorr soups are a traditional part of every dinner, as is some kind of dessert. If time permits, I'll bake cinnamon rolls or chocolate cake on my trail stove (see section on ovens, page 33), and later pig contentedly on popcorn and spiced tea. Otherwise, I rely on dried foods like Minute Rice, Instant Mashed Potatoes, noodles, and Bisquick. And for auto camping, where weight is no object, anything goes — that is, if it will fit in my 60 quart ice chest.

Munchies

Car campers will prey heavily on junk foods while hikers, bikers and canoeists will opt for more nutritious snacks, such as fruitcake, dehydrated fruit, popcorn, granola bars and mixed nuts. (Note: cashews have the highest nutritional value of the various nuts.)

Packing Suggestions

To eliminate confusion, package each meal for your group as a complete unit. Remove all unnecessary packaging to save as much weight and space as possible. I pack *"flowable solids,"* like Tang and baking mix in small Zip-lock bags which are encased in sturdy nylon bags. Breakable and crushable items like crackers and cheese go inside rigid cardboard containers. A cut down cereal box works fine, but a half-gallon milk carton is ideal. Later, in camp, you can use the milk carton for mixing Kool-Aid and puddings. Or shred it up for use as an emergency fire-starter.

Liquids are best carried in plastic bottles which have screw-cap lids. The original *"Nalgene"* polyethylene containers are most reliable, though they are expensive. Supermarket syrup and honey bottles work marginally well, if you replace their plastic pop-tops with rigid caps which won't accidentally release. Another solution is to melt the flip tops to a mass of flowable plastic in the burner of your stove.

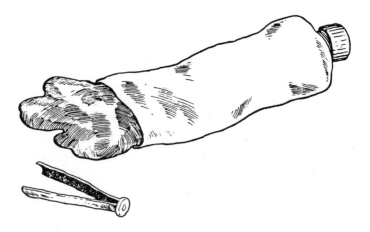

Figure 6-2. Food tubes are convenient, but not always reliable.

Most camping shops sell plastic food tubes which you fill with jam, honey or peanut butter. The tubes are filled from the open back end then clipped shut with a slotted plastic tube. You dispense the product just like toothpaste. Sounds great, but the units frequently fail — usually inside your pack. The mess that results is ... *"interesting."*

Each plastic-bagged meal should be placed into its own color-coded waterproof nylon sack. You'll save much pack groping at meal time if you adopt a color-coded system. I traditionally pack my breakfasts in green bags, my lunches in blue, and suppers in red. Since I don't like surprises, I label the contents of each sack on the outside with crayon.

If you pack your food in discreet, pre-measured units as I suggest, everything will be at hand. And, you'll never have to eat damp oatmeal!

Food Preparation Hints

Biscuits and cakes: Don't mix batter in a bowl: It's too messy. Instead, pre-measure the bake-stuff into a large plastic bag. Add water to the bag then knead its contents until the texture is right. Cut a slit in the bag bottom then squeeze (use the bag like a cake decorator) the contents into your awaiting oven. Voilá! No mess or waste. Burn the plastic bag.

Making popcorn: Making popcorn for large groups is a hassle, even if you have a large pot. Here's an easier way: As you complete each batch of popped corn, pour it into a large paper grocery sack (don't use a plastic bag — the hot corn will melt through it!). Season the corn and shake the bag to mix. Later, burn the bag.

Paper towels: Paper toweling is always handy on a campout. If you pack a half-dozen sheets of toweling with each meal, you won't have to search for the main roll when dishwashing time rolls around.

How to Prepare Freeze-Dried Foods
So They Always Taste Good

There's a notion that freeze-dried foods are awful. Not so. Prepare 'em right and they're just two steps below wonderful. Do it wrong, and ... ugh!

Take heart. Here's a foolproof method that won't let you down.

1. Read the directions but don't take them too seriously. What works at home on the range often fails in the field. Typical directions call for dumping everything into boiling water and simmering the brew for X minutes — a practice which usually results in overcooking one portion of the meal while undercooking another. If the freeze-dried meat comes out rubbery, while the noodles are pasty, you've done something wrong.

2. Separate the components of the food. Usually, there are two parts — a meat and a pasta or vegetable portion. Sometimes, there's a spice packet.

3. Add *20 percent more* water to the pot than the directions call for, and *add the meat portion only* to the cold water. Bring the water to a boil and add a healthy dash of *"All-spice."* See suggested recipe below:

Mix approximately equal amounts of these spices:
Oregano
Dash of onion powder
Marjoram
Dash of thyme
Seasoned salt and pepper mixture (I buy a commercial blend)

4. When the water boils, add the spice packet (if there is one) and allow the spices to simmer with the meat a full five minutes. If there is no spice packet, simply cook the meat for five minutes. *Then,* add the pasta or vegetable package and simmer everything for the length of time specified in the directions.

5. Remove the covered pot from the stove and set it aside for a few minutes. Now, eat and enjoy. All portions of the meal are thoroughly cooked and the taste is fully developed.

If you've ever cooked oriental foods in a wok, you'll understand why this *"time-layered"* method works so well. Throwing everything together simultaneously as recommended, usually produces glue, not stew!

Cookware

You can get along with about half as much cookware as you think you need. Two nesting pots, a coffee pot, fry pan, plastic bowls, insulated cups and spoons are sufficient for a party of four.

Don't waste your money on *"Trail Queen"* nested cooksets that contain useless items. Buy the pots you need and fill out the rest with materials from your kitchen. In the end you'll save weight, space and money, and enjoy real utility.

Ovens

If you plan to bake, you'll need an oven of some sort. Polished aluminum reflector ovens are traditional, but outdated in these days of small fires and trail stoves. My vote goes to the *"Jello mold oven,"* which is nothing more than a large ring aluminum Jello mold and a high cover. Jello mold ovens will work on any trail stove and will produce quality bake stuff in about the same time as your home oven.

To use the Jello mold for baking on your stove ...

1.   Grease the mold and pour your bake stuff into the outside ring. Decrease the suggested amount of water by up to one-fourth for faster baking.

2.   Bring the stove to its normal operating temperature then reduce the heat to the lowest possible blue-flame setting. Center the Jello mold over the burner head, top it with a high cover (necessary to provide sufficient room for the bake goods to rise) and relax. Cooking times are nearly identical to those suggested in the baking directions.

The triple-pan method of baking on your stove is another alternative ...

You'll need two nesting skillets, a high cover, and a half dozen small nails or stones.

1.   Evenly scatter the nails or stones onto the surface of the large (bottom) frying pan.

2.   Place your bake stuff into the small frying pan and set it on top of the nails (the two pans must be separated by nails or stones to prevent burning).

3.   Cover the unit and place it on your stove. Use the lowest possible blue-flame setting.

Warning: Don't use this method with a thin aluminum skillet on the bottom; you'll burn a hole right through it!

Pitfalls of Winter Cooking

Your body burns much more energy in winter than in summer, so rely heavily on foods which are rich in fat and carbohydrates (fats contain about twice as many calories per pound as carbohydrates and are the body's major source of stored energy). Unfortunately, some fat rich foods which are summer favorites don't work well in winter. A good example is peanut butter. Try chiseling peanut butter out of a poly bottle at 20 below zero and you'll see why.

Cheese, another high fat food, doesn't fare too well either — mainly because it tastes like candle wax when near frozen. However, cheese melts nicely into any hot food.

Salami (any sausage) on the other hand, tastes good frozen or thawed. You can use it as is or to fortify soups and freeze-dried entrees.

Food preparation tips: It takes much longer to cook foods in winter than in summer, so increase cooking times substantially. *"Cook-in-the-bag"* entrees like those made by *"Mountain House"* will cook at low temperatures if you set the boiling water filled food bag into a covered pot of near boiling water for ten minutes. This procedure will assure complete cooking and eliminate a dirty pot.

Since an icy wind can rob heat from a thin aluminum pot almost as fast as your stove can produce it, keep your pots covered and sheltered. A good procedure is to simply burrow the kitchen below the surface of the snow.

Washing dishes: Some winter campers advise cleaning dishes with snow (a messy procedure). I've found it's better to wash them the traditional way in boiling water (no soap). I wear light wool gloves under plastic coated cotton ones to keep my hands toasty warm and dry throughout the experience. Bacteria are inactive in frigid temperatures so it's not necessary to rinse and dry your cookware. A little grease on your bowl won't hurt you — as long as it's *your* grease. It follows that each camper *must* have his/her own bowl, cup and spoon.

Bowls and such: Give some thought to the selection of plastic cups and bowls. Plastic which is brittle in the store may shatter on the winter trail. Surprisingly, inexpensive, flexible plastics are often superior to stronger but more brittle, expensive ones.

Keep your cooking and eating utensils secured in a compartmented fabric roll so you won't lose them in a snow drift. And pack spices in film containers, not salt shakers which gum up.

Cold feet: The cook spends considerable time just standing around, so some sort of insulation underfoot is essential. An 18-inch square of half-inch thick closed cell foam is ideal. I suggest you don't use your foam sleeping pad for this purpose as your night time comfort depends on keeping it absolutely dry.

To light up your life: Winter days are short so you may need to depend on artificial light for cooking. Flashlights are generally unsuitable in sub-zero temperatures, and candle lanterns don't produce enough light. Your best bet is a miner's headlamp (the type that takes four D-cells). If you use alkaline batteries and keep the battery pack inside your parka for warmth, you'll have enough light to last a week on the typical cross-country ski trip.

To keep liquids from freezing: Liquids freeze less rapidly if they're capped and submerged in the snow. Freezing begins at the air interface of a liquid so store beverage filled poly bottles *upside down.* This way, you're less apt to experience the difficulty of removing a frozen bottle cap.

A Thermos bottle may save more than its weight in stove fuel: I fill my Thermos as soon as the tea is done to save re-heating it later. If there's a campfire, I set the Thermos near it for warmth. And when I retire, the vacuum bottle goes into the bag with me to ensure a ready hot drink come morning.

Major cooking dangers: When it's 20 below and you're dressed in a down parka and double shell mittens, performing simple chores like turning down the stove or lifting a pot cover, takes on new dimensions. A real danger centers around use of the stove. For example, I once burned a large hole in the sleeve of an expensive down parka when I passed my arm too close to the stove burner. Sub-zero clothing is a good insulator so you may not detect a burn until much of your outfit has gone up in flames. Be *extremely* careful around stoves when you're bundled up.

Incidentally, use care when handling stove fuels (gasoline and kerosene) in cold weather. Liquid fuels freeze at much lower temperatures than water so you're set for instant frostbite should you inadvertently spill some on bare hands. For safety sake, handle fuel bottles while wearing gloves!

Leftovers: A major summer problem — what to do with uneaten food — is minimized in winter. I simple scoop frozen food waste into a Zip-lock bag and carry it along until I have the opportunity to burn it. Some winter travelers leave uneaten food on the snow *"for the animals"* — a practice not approved by national park and forest service personnel. Careless food habits — especially in winter when natural foods are scarce — might turn an ordinarily shy critter into a bold nasty one. Wild animals are perfectly capable of finding their own dinner (in any season!) without man's help.

Old hands at summer camping should have no trouble adapting to the subtle differences of the winter kitchen. The important thing is to experiment with foods and cooking procedures *before* you take to the winter woods.

7. STORMPROOFING THE TENT

For two days, the TV blasted warnings of the coming storm. Just south of us there were winds of 40 miles an hour and ice cold rain. By all reports, the weather system would hit us sometime Saturday. Nonetheless, we refused to alter our plans — the rule in Scouting being, *"you never cancel a campout!"*

When we pulled into the campground, the sky was already darkening. Scoutmaster Chic Sheridan and I studied the terrain: We figured we had maybe an hour to rig a snug camp, so we went to work immediately.

There were three spots for tents: The lower level — located about two feet above the river, would provide room for a half dozen tents. The wide flat terrace farther up could take four. And the gentle rolling hill top could hold two or three.

An upward glance revealed that the hill was out of the question, as it was already occupied by a state-of-the-art nylon dome. Granted, we could probably crowd one or two scout tents along side, but the positioning would be only temporary: The first stormy blast would send them crashing down. No, the hill was simply a bad location.

On the lower level near the river, there was plenty of space for our five tents, but we declined the option, knowing full well the dangers of a major storm and a rising river.

"Over there," called Chic, pointing to the center terrace. *"Get 'em up boys!"* Now, the apparent disorder of before came to a halt.

Suddenly, everyone seemed to know exactly what he was doing. Within minutes, tents were pitched and battened for the worst.

The scout tents were primitive compared to the exotic dome on the hill — just old but solid canvas wall tents with sewn-in floors and a single vertical pole at each end. Nonetheless, we knew they'd stand quite a blow if properly rigged.

First, the boys placed an oversize 4-mil plastic groundsheet inside each tent, taking care to fold the edges of the plastic well up the sidewalls. This would protect the sleeping bags of those boys who slept along the perimeter. Next, they attached two stout guylines to each tent peak (Figure 7-1) and fanned them out to

Figure 7-1. Storm-proofing the tent.

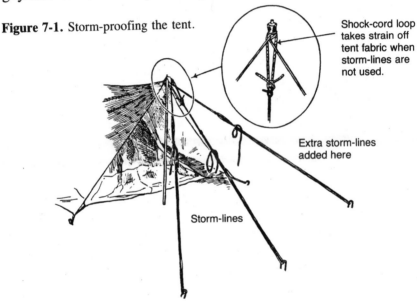

Shock-cord loop takes strain off tent fabric when storm-lines are not used.

Extra storm-lines added here

Storm-lines

stakes below. Each tent was now held firm by *three* taut ropes at each end. Years before, I had installed loops of quarter-inch shock cord at the peak of each tent to absorb the stress normally reserved for the stitching and fabric.

"Run storm lines off the side, too! And weight the windward stakes with big rocks," I called. The younger scouts followed the example of the older ones, who scampered about and barked commands. Meticulously, the boys tied lengths of parachute cord to the nylon loops we'd sewn to the tent hems. Now, instead of just three stakes per sidewall, there were five. The view from the hill looked like Charlotte's web. Hopefully, it would be as secure.

"Okay, boys," I shouted. *"Let's get two rain flies (tarps) up. Pair 'em off a common ridge. Get on it!"*

Again, the fir began to fly. First, a drum-tight rope was strung between two trees. Then two boys tied the ridge of the tarp while two more staked the tail. Coiled loops of parachute cord tied to the main face of the tarp were pulled free and staked out to nearby trees (Figure 7-2) — a procedure that required less than three minutes. When the first fly was set, a second was mated, A-frame fashion along side. No need to search for extra cord or stakes — everything required was in the nylon bag which contained each tarp (see RIGGING THE TARP, page 40).

Ten minutes later we crowded under the low slung flies, ready to prepare a gourmet supper and laugh at the whims of nature. I fired up the big Optimus 111B stove and put on the coffee pot while Chic greeted the three college kids who'd dropped in to comment on our show.

"That your dome up there?" I questioned, pointing to the hill.

"Yeah," said one of the boys proudly.

"You know you're right in the path of the storm," I quipped.

"No biggie," was the reply. *"They say it'll take 50 mile an hour winds."*

"Hope you're right: The test will come any time now."

With that, one of the boys poked gentle fun at our canvas menagerie, slyly suggesting that the wind gods would probably flatten everything by morning.

I just smiled: We knew better!

Within the hour it began. Innocently at first, with a light drizzle that lasted for an hour. Then the storm intensified; soon rain fell in thick sheets, driven by winds of 40 miles an hour.

Once, during the night, I sat up in despair and hugged the rear pole, certain the tent was about to come crashing down. But it held fast, testimony to our weatherproofing.

We awoke the following morning to the scene of disaster. There were downed trees and debris everywhere. One of our tents was partially collapsed, though the boys inside were still fast asleep. I stole a skyward glance towards the hill top. The dome? It was gone, and so were the boys who'd occupied it. All that remained was a swatch of blue nylon tangled in branches high above.

Chic and I exchanged smug glances: We'd weathered the storm!

Let's review the procedures for effective stormproofing:

1. *Always* use a plastic ground cloth *inside* your tent. Water which wicks through worn floor fabric and/or seams will be trapped by the ground sheet. *Never* put the ground cloth under the tent floor!

2. Attach loops of shock-cord or bands cut from inner tubes to all guylines. Shock-cords take up the wind stress normally reserved for seams and fittings. Even a badly sewn, poorly reinforced tent can be used in severe weather if it's outfitted with shock-cords.

3. Know the shortcomings of your tent and correct them. Reinforce questionable seams and add additional stake loops if you need them.

4. When high winds threaten, run three guylines off each tent peak. Note: Tents which are completely self-supporting (like the Eureka Timberline and most domes) will blow down if you don't guy them securely.

Rigging the Tarp

Stormproofing your tent is only half the solution to keeping dry in rain. The other part is having a dry place to cook and relax. A large (10 foot by 10 foot) nylon tarp pitched between trees or suspended from guyed poles will provide ample protection for four.

For a quick rainproof shelter that won't flap in the wind, try this rigging procedure:

1. String a tight line about six feet high between two trees. Use two half-hitches at one end of the rope and a *"power-cinch"* with a quick release knot, at the other (see Chapter 8 for a review of knots and hitches).

2. Tie one edge of the fly to the line. This will distribute the wind load among several points along the fly. Wrap the corner ties around the line a few times before you tie them to produce friction so the fly won't slide inward along the line when it's buffeted by wind.

3. Stake down the back end of the fly, then guy the center to an overhanging limb or rope strung overhead. If this is impossible,

Figure 7-2. Customizing the Rain Tarp: Add ties to all the grommets and sew five equally spaced loops to the face. This will allow you to pitch the tarp in a variety of geometric configurations.

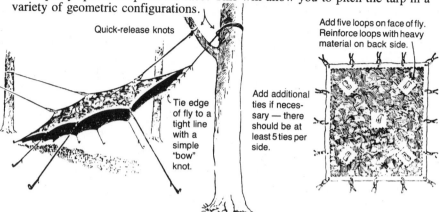

Quick-release knots

Tie edge of fly to a tight line with a simple "bow" knot.

Add additional ties if necessary — there should be at least 5 ties per side.

Add five loops on face of fly. Reinforce loops with heavy material on back side.

prop out the center from the inside with a pole. Don't try this unless you've sewn a protective pole patch to the fly. Without one, you'll stretch the fly out of shape or tear it. And don't use Visklamps (ball and garter devices) to pitch a fly. Visklamps stretch and abrade fabric unmercifully.

4. Guy the sides as the terrain permits.

Be sure you complete all knots and hitches with quick-release loops, as explained in chapter eight, so you can change or drop the outfit at a moment's notice. When severe winds threaten, simply lower one or both ends of the ridge rope.

Packing the fly: Pack your fly in a nylon bag, along with 60 feet of parachute cord (cut into 15 foot lengths) and a half dozen wire tent stakes. This will greatly simplify pitching.

For large groups, pair two tarps at the ridge. Overlap one tarp so there'll be no leaks.

When all day rains come to stay, it may be necessary to move the campfire under the fly — a procedure which requires raising the tail hem a foot off the ground to provide *"flow through"* ventilation. Without this ventilation, you'll do a smoke dance inside. Raising the hem necessarily requires unstaking the fly and meticulously guying each point to distant trees.

Snug Camp

Campcraft books are rich with advice on *"choosing the right campsite."* But most commentary is a waste of space since even a rank novice knows better than to pitch his tent in a depression, on unlevel ground, or in a bog. Since it's unethical (and often illegal) to clear trees and brush and to *"improve"* sites by trenching around tents, you usually have to take what's available and make the best of it. Forest Service and Park personnel don't always establish campsites with an eye for the lay of the land. Most of the time, I'm overjoyed just to find a level place to set my tent. After that, I worry about creature comforts like a south facing slope, proximity to good water, effective drainage, shade and wind protection, a nice view, etc.

Nonetheless, here's one bit of advice worth repeating. *"Don't camp in a meadow or flat mossy area."* Cold damp air settles in meadows, and moss acts like a giant sponge: It traps water for miles around. If it rains while you're camped on moss, you'll be elbow deep in water by morning. Even the most watertight groundcloth won't save you under these conditions.

Bears, Beasts and Flying Critters
Bears

There are two views about bears: One suggests that all bruins are timid and will run at the first smell of you. The other warns that bears are mankillers and advises you to bring big guns!

In-between these extremes is the real truth. Nearly all bears are timid and will ordinarily stay away from humans. But there are a few crazy bears, and these must be given a wide berth. The problem is not so much in telling which bears are insane, as it is in knowing when it's time to stop pretending *"you're boss,"* and instead get out of the way.

Here are the generally agreed upon rules for staying out of bear trouble:

1. If you come face to face with a bear, *don't* run! Talk gently but firmly, and stretch out your arms so you'll appear big. As you talk, slowly back off. In all likelihood, the bear will do the same. Yelling and screaming, as advised by some authorities, may or may not produce positive results. If the bear's a female with cubs, this action may provoke her into a charge.

2. If the bear runs towards you, climb the nearest tree. If there are no trees, hold your ground and ball up into a fetal position and

Figure 7-3. Bears are very adept at getting food packs out of trees.

play dead. I was once *"charged"* by three grizzlies in the arctic tundra. When they were 100 feet away, I curled into a tight ball, hands clasped behind my neck, and prayed. They came within a dozen feet, and sensing I was no threat, loped merrily away. The procedure works!

Black bears are usually very predictable. Grizzlies and polar bears are not! Each bear must be treated with the full knowledge that you are a guest in his neighborhood and *he* is in charge. Remember this, and you'll have no trouble with bears.

Protecting your food from bears: The common advice is to hang food packs in a tree or suspend them from a tight rope strung between two trees. Frankly, I think this is a mistake. Bears are creatures of habit; they quickly learn where, and in what, campers keep their food. Moreover, in every campsite there is usually only one or two trees with limbs which are high enough to discourage bears. Once the bruins learn the location of these *"bear trees,"* they'll check them faithfully every night. And they become very adept at getting down whatever is up there!

It's not always the smell of food which attracts bears. Often, the sight of the food container (pack or tin can) is enough. For this reason, I never put my food packs in trees. Instead, I take them *out of the campsite area* and set them in the woods. On several occasions, a curious blackie has strolled through my camp, checked out the *"bear tree,"* sniffed around awhile, and left — while in the shadows just a few dozen feet away, there sat a pack filled with gourmet delights.

If a bear can't smell or see your food, he won't get it. Line your food packs with plastic and keep a clean camp and you won't have trouble with wild animals!

Insects: Everyone knows that repellents are essential on most camping trips. But the color of your clothes is also important. Insects (especially mosquitoes) are attracted to dark colors, notably navy blue. Powder-blue, yellow, white, and most greens and reds are neutral. The light colors may, in fact, have a mild repellent effect.

If you're camping with children, choose a mild cream repellent rather than a more effective one which is high in *"DEET"* (N-N Diethyl-metatoluamide). Strong repellents may burn sensitive young skin. And oh yes, keep repellents away from plastics: These products will instantly dissolve eye glasses, polypropylene underwear, and the handles of Swiss army knives!

Ecological Concerns

Food leftovers should be bagged in plastic and packed out of the woods. When this is impractical, the best method of disposal is burning. Even soupy foodstuffs will burn if you add them a little at a time to a hot fire.

Burn all garbage *completely,* being sure to pick aluminum foil out of the flames. Burn out tin cans and flatten them with the back of your handaxe or a rock...and pack them out!

Fish entrails *should not* be thrown into a waterway where they will increase bacteria levels and reduce the supply of oxygen for fish. Instead, bury viscera *four to eight inches deep,* as far as possible from the campsite. This relatively shallow depth is best for decomposition and also minimizes the possibility of it being dug up by animals. If there's only an inch or two of soil cover available, weight remains with a heavy rock or log.

Human waste too, should be buried four to eight inches deep (an aluminum tube with one end flattened makes a good shovel). Toilet paper and sanitary napkins should be burned as these items require a full year or more to degrade.

And *please* don't throw food (or anything else!) in Forest Service box latrines or chemical toilets. Bears commonly upset latrines to get at food. The mess that results is indescribable.

Dishes should be washed 100 feet away from a water source. Greasy dishwater is best poured into a small hole in the ground and covered with a few inches of soil. It should go without saying that you should never bathe (with soap) in any waterway!

Water Purification

If you value your health, you'll get your drinking water only from "*approved*" sources, or you'll treat it or carry it with you.

I confess to laziness in this respect. I despise the taste of chemically treated water; I don't like to mess with filters, and at eight pounds per gallon, I'll seldom carry more than a canteen full of water. Usually, I obtain my drinking water from a lake or river, though I'm very careful where I get it. Here are the guidelines I religiously follow:

1. Go well away from any shoreline to get drinking water. If you're camping at a spot that is frequented by man or animals, go upstream of the source to get your water. On lakes, a minimum of 100 feet from shore is recommended — and the farther out you go the better.

2. Decay organisms (bacteria, protozoans and fungi) generally prefer the shallows, so the deeper your water source, the better.

3. Avoid any water which has a greenish tinge. It contains algae and is usually loaded with microorganisms.

4. Don't take water from backwaters and stagnant areas. These are breeding places for microorganisms.

5. Don't drink any water that has been contaminated by wastes from a paper mill. Secure your water from incoming streams instead.

6. Don't take water near beaver dams or lodges. Beaver are the favored host of Giardia lamblia — a small protozoan that will make you plenty sick. The disease (called Giardiasis) is characterized by severe diarrhea, cramps, nausea, gas and vomiting. Incubation time is generally one or two weeks, though some people have gone as long as two months without developing symptoms. If untreated, Giardiasis may go on for years. The disease is not at all easy to diagnose.

Field methods of water treatment...

1. *Boiling:* Most organisms are killed instantly when water reaches a rolling boil. A one minute boil is usually adequate, except in problem areas or at high altitudes.

2. *Portable filters:* The vacuum operated, portable filters sold at camping shops will produce quality water, but they're very slow to use. And not all filters will remove Giardia.

3. *Chemicals:* Chemicals which release iodine or chlorine are available in tablet form from most pharmacies and camping shops. Generally, iodine is more effective than chlorine, especially on Giardia. However, neither compound works very well in cold or cloudy water.

Despite new chemicals and scientific filters, boiling remains the most reliable method for treating drinking water.

Hypothermia — Killer of the Unprepared

The morning begins with a golden sun; by noon scattered clouds of twisted gray appear low on the horizon. Within the hour, an icy drizzle falls. Curiously, you look skyward, hopeful the discomfort will soon pass. But it doesn't. The rain continues. You snug the hood of your well worn rain parka in hopes of discouraging the chilling drizzle which has already soaked your cotton T-shirt and blue jeans. Soon, you begin to shiver, slightly at first, then uncontrollably. Ultimately, your speech thickens and you lose orientation. It's hard now to tell up from down, right from left. One minute you're walking drone-like down the muddy trail, the next, you're on your knees groping.

Total collapse comes an hour later. Suddenly, your sense of feel and awareness is gone. Shivering ceases, muscles become rigid; the once tender, pink skin becomes puffy white. You have penetrated the danger zone. Without help, you'll drift further into oblivion, towards death — the final goal.

Fortunately, knowledgeable friends are nearby and in command. Within minutes a tent is pitched and foam pads and bedding are placed inside. Wet clothes are stripped from your inanimate body and you are rushed to the awaiting sleeping bag where you are sandwiched — skin to skin — between two friends. Additional sleeping bags and parkas are pulled from their stuff sacks and piled over you. Nearby, someone struggles with a trail stove — hot soup is on the way.

The condition persists for many minutes, but ultimately your frigid body is re-warmed and you are able to sit up and talk intelligently. Now that you can swallow, you are given gentle sips of hot broth and are cheered back to your former state.

You are very lucky. Without such well directed, quick assistance, you surely would have died!

In the old days, they called it *"exposure sickness."* Now, the technical term is *"hypothermia."* But the cause — and symptoms — are the same. Hypothermia is a lowering of the body's core temperature. It may result from being plunged into cold water (immersion hypothermia), or from slow chilling, as in the above example.

The onset of hypothermia occurs when body temperature drops

below about 95 degrees Fahrenheit. As blood is rushed to the vital
organs, chilling spreads throughout the body. This is accompanied
by clumsiness, slurred speech, and loss of judgment. Coma and
death may occur with a few hours if the body temperature is not
raised.

Most hypothermics are unaware of what is happening to them
and will maintain an *"I'm okay!"* attitude to the bitter end. It's up
to other members of the party to observe the signals and take
appropriate action.

Treatment for hypothermia consists of removing wet clothes
and sandwiching the victim between two people in a sleeping bag,
alá the illustrative example. Radiant heat from a fire may be used
to speed the warming process, and is probably the quickest way to
warm a hypothermic under typical field conditions. Be careful
though: intense heat may burn the sensitive skin of the victim.

Hypothermia is physically and emotionally draining. Victims
should be allowed to rest for a full day following the experience.

Your best protection against hypothermia is prevention. Select
reliable rain gear and choose clothing which insulates well when
wet. Wool is the traditional fabric, though polypropylene and pile
work as well. Wet cotton literally wisks heat from the skin, so this
fabric should never be worn in tricky weather. As mentioned, blue
jeans are the worst thing you can wear in the backcountry.

Finally, keep the calories flowing while you hike. Constant
nibbling on candy/nuts/granola, etc., will keep the temperature of
your *"furnace"* high. If you get wet, stop immediately and change
clothes. Many have died from hypothermia while clinging to the
belief that they were *"saving their dry clothes for camp."*

8. ROPEMANSHIP

Given enough rope…and time, anyone can rig a snug camp. Add a knife, and anyone can cut one down. Between these extremes are a small number of elite outdoorspeople who can match the right knot to the job at hand — and untie it instantly the morning after an all night rain. Stroll through a wooded campground at season's end and count the number of tightly knotted cords you see hanging hopelessly from the vegetation and you'll understand the importance of *"ropemanship."*

Outdoor handbooks define dozens of knots, most of which are quite useless in the woods. In reality, all you need to know are two knots and two hitches. Learn these well, and you'll be at home in any situation, even those which require some rescue work.

Old timers will note the conspicuous absence of the square knot and tautline hitch. Except for limited first-aid applications, the square knot is worthless; and the infamous tautline-hitch — so useful in the days of cotton tents and manila rope — has now been replaced by the much more powerful and versatile *"power-cinch."*

The Double Half-Hitch
(two half-hitches)

The double half-hitch is useful for tying a rope to a tree, as for a clothesline or to rig a tarp. The knot is very secure and tends to tighten itself when a load is applied. If you want to get this knot

Figure 8-1. Double Half-hitch:

out quickly, finish it with a quick-release loop as shown in Figure 8-6.

The Sheet Bend

Use the sheet bend for tying two ropes together. The knot works well even when rope sizes are dissimilar. The sheet-bend is about the only knot that can be used to join the ends of slippery polypropylene rope.

A friend once won five dollars when he fixed a broken water-ski tow-rope with this knot. When the tow-line snapped, the owner of the ski boat bet my friend he couldn't tie the two ends of the slick polypropylene rope together tightly enough to hold. No problem. My friend won the bet and skied the remainder of the day on the repaired line.

Figure 8-2. Sheet Bend:

It's important that the free ends of the sheet bend be on the same side as shown in Figure 8-2. The knot will work if the ends are opposite, but it will be less secure.

The Bowline

Here's an absolutely secure knot which won't slip regardless of the load applied. The bowline is the most important knot for mountain climbing. Use it whenever you want to put a nonslip loop on the end of a line...or around your waist.

Figure 8-3. Bowline:

Beginners are often told to make the bowline by forming a loop, or *"rabbit hole."* The rabbit (free end of the rope) comes up through the hole, around the tree (opposite or long end of the rope shown in Figure 8-3) and back down the hole. The knot will slip a few inches before it tightens, so allow an extra long free end.

Power-Cinch

This ingenious hitch works like a winch with a 2:1 mechanical advantage. Use it to secure the lines of a tent to a stake or tree, or to rig a drum-tight clothesline in camp. The power-cinch is the hitch of choice whenever you need a secure tie-down. Carrying canoes on car tops, lashing furniture into the bed of pickup trucks, tying tents and sleeping bags to aluminum pack frames, are all useful applications of this versatile hitch.

Begin the power-cinch by forming the loop shown in Figure

52

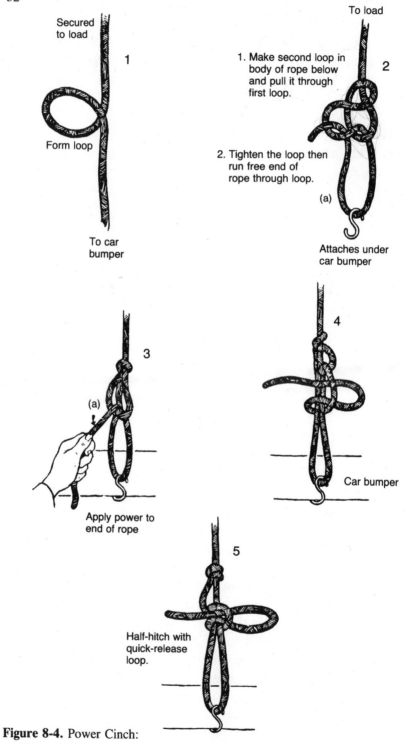

Figure 8-4. Power Cinch:

Figure 8-5. Secure your tent to a tree or stack with a power cinch.

8-4, step 1. Pull the loop through as in step 2. It's important that the loop be formed *exactly* as shown. The loop will look okay if you make it backwards, but it won't work.

If the loop is formed as in step 2, a simple tug on the rope will eliminate it. This is preferable to the common practice of tying a knot in the loop, which, after being exposed to a load, is almost impossible to get out.

If you're tying a load in place on top of a car, tie one end of the rope to the load and snap the steel hook on the other end of the rope to the car's bumper — or, if you're using a car top carrier, run the rope from bar to bar, using two half-hitches on one side, a power-cinch on the other. Run the free end of the rope (a) through the loop in the power-cinch (step 2), and apply power to the free end. You've created a pulley with a 2:1 mechanical advantage.

Complete the hitch by securing a double-half hitch around the body of the rope, or use a *"quick-release"* loop as illustrated.

Figure 8-6. Secure your stuff sacks with a quick-release loop.

The Quick-Release Loop

There's nothing more frustrating than untying a bunch of tight knots when you're breaking camp in the morning. If you end your knots with a *"quick-release"* loop like that illustrated in Figure 8-4, step 5, you'll be able to untie your lines with a single pull.

Form the quick-release feature by running the free end of the rope back through the completed knot — same as making a *"bow"* when tying your shoes.

Use a simple overhand knot with a quick-release loop to seal the stuff sacks which contain your sleeping bag and personal gear. The plastic *"cord-locks"* sold for this purpose are for people who don't know how to tie effective quick-release knots.

9. ON COURSE TO MAKING ROUTE DECISIONS

Every year, members of the famed Appalachian Mountain Club rescue scores of lost hikers and campers, most of which have a compass in their pocket when they're found. If asked, *"Why didn't you use your compass to find your way back to camp?"* They invariably reply: *"I tried ... but I didn't know how.".* When AMC rescuers question why these people insist on carrying an instrument they don't know how to use, an overwhelming majority respond by stating that *"everyone should carry a compass in case they get lost!"*

So much for logic.

Fortunately, anyone can learn the basics of backcountry navigation in a few hours, if he or she is willing to make the effort.

Equipment First
The Map

Except for going in a straight line, a compass is useless without a map. Any map — even a photocopied State Park trail guide — is better than no map at all. A map provides the directions you need: The compass is merely the tool that enables you to follow them!

Get the best topographic maps available. These can be purchased from two major sources:

To order United States maps, write to:
    U.S. Geological Survey
    Map Distribution Section
    Federal Center
    Denver, Colorado 80225

To order Canadian maps, write to:
    Canada Map Office
    615 Booth St.
    Ottawa, Ontario, Canada K1A OE9

For advance trip planning it's best to write the appropriate
map office and request a free INDEX TO TOPOGRAPHIC MAPS.
These indexes tell what maps are in print, in what scale, and the
cost. Rather than bore you with the complexities of the many scales
available, suffice it to say that the larger the scale, the more useful
the map.
    In American maps, your best bet is to get 1:24,000 (one inch
on the map equals 24,000 inches — or 2,000 feet — on the ground)
maps. When traveling in Canada, the 1:50,000 (1 1/4 inches to
the mile) quadrangles are ideal.
    When maps arrive, outline your route and tick off the proposed
mileage. This way, you won't attempt to cover more distance than
you're capable of. Finally, waterproof your maps with a chemical
preparation. I've had good luck with *"Stormproof"* (write the Martensen Co., P.O. Box 261, Williamsburg, VA 23185), and
"Thompson's Water Seal" — an industrial strength compound that's
used for sealing concrete block. You'll find Thompson's Water
Seal on the shelves of most hardware stores in aerosol cans and
tins. I buy it by the quart and apply it to maps and journals with
a polyurethane foam varnish brush. The product also does a fine
job of waterproofing hats and clothing.
    Water-resistant maps should be further protected by sealing
them inside a plastic map case.

Interpreting Contour Lines

You can't appreciate the value of a good map until you understand how to interpret contour lines. These basics will get you through:

1. Contour lines are light brown lines on a map which connect points of *equal* elevation. Thus, closely spaced lines indicate lots of elevation change, whereas wide-spaced lines show the opposite (Figure 9-1 and 9-2).

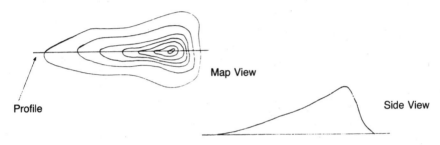

Figure 9-1. Basic contours of a long sloping hill that gives a rough idea of interval spacing. *Note* the significant drop on the right side of the hill and the gentle slope at left.

2. The closed or *"vee"* end of a contour line always points upstream (see Figure 9-2).

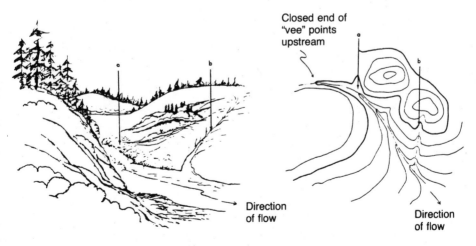

Figure 9-2. Stream (b) flows into river (a).

3. Where contour lines cross or run very close together, you'll find an abrupt drop — a falls or canyon.

4. The vertical distance between contour lines is called the CONTOUR INTERVAL, and its value is given in the map legend. It *is not* the same for all maps.

5. The larger the contour interval, the less clear are the characteristics of the land. In short, a map whose CI = 10 feet, gives a much clearer picture of the topography than one whose CI = 100 feet. Note that foreign maps give all information in *meters,* and these will need to be converted to feet to be meaningful to most Americans.

If you study Figures 9-1 and 9-2, these rules will become obvious.

The Compass

There are a number of different compass types, but only the versatile Orienteering model, pioneered by Silva, makes much sense for traveling the backcountry. Orienteering models have built-in protractors which allow you to quickly and accurately compute direction and scale distance *without first orienting the map to north.*

Figure 9-3. The "Orienteering" compass permits computation of true directions from a map *without* orienting the map to north.

This means you can define a precise direction to the nearest degree while hustling down a wilderness trail! Additionally, your direction of travel is physically set on the compass by turning a dial. There's nothing to remember and nothing to write down.

Basics First

First, learn the *compass rose* (Figure 9-4) and memorize the bearings (degree readings) of the eight principal points. Before you determine the direction of travel from a map with the protractor function of your compass, ask yourself: *"What's the approximate bearing to my objective?"* Make certain your guestimate roughly agrees with the bearing you computed from your map. This procedure will eliminate the two most common compass errors — the 180 degree error (you go north instead of south) and the 100 degree error (you travel at 240 degrees instead of 140 or 340). It's amazing how flustered you get when you're uncertain of where you are. In fact, lost persons have been known to read their compasses backwards.

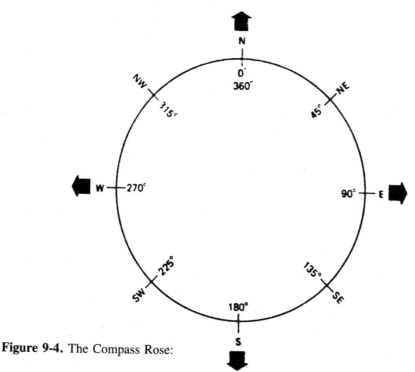

Figure 9-4. The Compass Rose:

If you know the approximate direction of travel *before* you read your compass, you'll eliminate all errors which result when transferring information from the map to the ground.

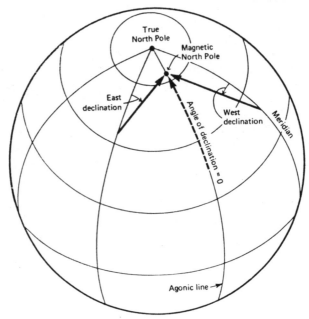

Figure 9-5. Compass Declination: The Angular Difference between *True* North and *Magnetic* North (the direction the compass points).

Declination

A compass needle points to magnetic north, not to true north, and this angular difference, called *declination*, must be considered whenever you use your compass (see Figures 9-5 and 9-6). In the eastern United States, the declination is westerly; in the western United States, it is easterly. If you live right on the imaginary line which goes through both true and magnetic north poles (called the *agonic* line) your declination will be zero.

In the northeast, the compass needle points more than 20 degrees west of true north, while in the far west, it errs by as much as 21 degrees east. Since one degree of compass error equals 92 feet per mile of ground error, this difference must be taken into account when you navigate.

Maps are always drawn in their true perspective, so any bearing you compute off them with the protractor function of your compass (no magnetic needle) will be a *true geographic direction*. This true — or map — bearing must be changed to a magnetic bearing to be set on your compass. There are two ways to make the conversion:

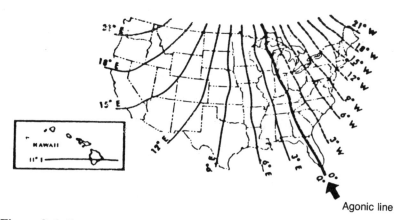

Agonic line

Figure 9-6. Standard Declination Chart:

First, buy a compass which has a mechanical device for offsetting the difference. Second, apply the rhyme, *"Declination east, compass least (subtract east declination from your map direction)."* Or, *"Declination west, compass best (add west declination to your map direction)."*

It's beyond the scope of this chapter to present a thorough investigation of wilderness navigation. If you want to learn more, see my books, THE NEW WILDERNESS CANOEING & CAMPING, and CANOEING WILD RIVERS. An excellent treatise on land navigation — which includes significant practice work — will be found in BE EXPERT WITH MAP AND COMPASS, by Bjorn Kjellstrom.

APPENDIX 1

MAIL ORDER SOURCES
OF QUALITY EQUIPMENT

Note: The companies listed below are those with which I've person-
ally done business. Quality of equipment and service is first-rate!

L.L. Bean, Inc.
Freeport, Maine 04033
    An uncommonly nice company which still does business in
the old world tradition. L.L. Bean is your best source of outdoor
wear and footgear. The famous "Maine Hunting Shoe" is the most
popular field boot in the world. Free catalog.

Recreational Equipment, Inc.
1525 11th Ave.
Seattle, Washington 98122
    REI is a co-op. You pay a few dollars to join and you receive
a yearly dividend (about ten percent) on your purchases. The co-op
specializes in mountaineering/backpacking equipment but also has
a wide selection of outdoor clothing and general camping items.

Cabela's Inc.
P.O. Box 199
812 Thirteenth Ave.
Sidney, Nebraska 69162
    A wide variety (and quality) of equipment. Good prices, fast
service. Extraordinary buys are sometimes possible.

Indiana Camp Supply, Inc.
P.O. Box 211, 1001 Lillian Street
Hobart, Indiana 46342

Best source of medical supplies (they specialize in hard-to-get items for the medical emergency) and freeze-dried foods. Good selection of high-tech and traditional camping items. Overnight delivery — fastest in the trade.

Campmor
810 Route 17 North
P.O. Box 997
Paramus, New Jersey 07653-0997

An incredibly complete catalog of outdoor gear. Everything from packs and tents to fabrics for repair are included. Good service, low prices.

Forestry Suppliers, Inc.
205 West Rankin St.
Jackson, Mississippi 39204

Your most complete source of forestry and surveying equipment — map aids, clear plastic for covering maps, compasses, etc. Also, lots of good knives, saws, and axes. Traditional camping equipment, too.

Cooke Custom Sewing
1544 Osborne Rd. N.E.
Fridley, Minnesota 55432

Outstanding pile and fleece outerwear, internal frame and soft packs, custom fabric spray covers for canoes, and hard-to-get specialty items for winter camping. Cooke Custom Sewing sews from their own proven patterns. Highly usable outdoor gear — no yuppie stuff. Also, custom sewing to your specs.

Martensen Company, Inc.
P.O. Box 261
Williamsburg, Virginia 23185

Liquid waterproofing material for maps.

Duluth Tent & Awning, Inc.
P.O. Box 16024
1610 W. Superior St.
Duluth, Minnesota 55816-0024
Your most complete source of canvas products, including Duluth packs for canoeing and traditional canvas camping and hunting tents. Duluth Tent & Awning will repair or customize tents and tarps.

Fast Bucksaw Co.
110 East 5th St.
Hastings, Minnesota 55033
Makers of what is, in my opinion, the best folding saw made.

Sierra West
6 East Yanonali St.
Santa Barbara, California 93101
A variety of well made clothing items. Sierra West has one of the best open-cell foam sleeping pads around.

The Ski Hut
P.O. Box 309
1615 University Ave.
Berkeley, California 94701
The Ski Hut manufacturers Trailwise equipment, made famous by Colin Fletcher in his book, *The Complete Walker.* They carry superb down-filled sleeping bags and outerwear as well as a good selection of general camping products. Ski Hut is known for its exquisite tailoring and fine workmanship on sleeping bags and parkas.

INDEX